Meet me at™

GAYLORD OPRYLAND

Meet me at
GAYLORD OPRYLAND

STORIED HISTORY AND TIMELESS IMAGES FROM NASHVILLE'S
GAYLORD OPRYLAND RESORT AND CONVENTION CENTER

Mary Lawson
Editor

Historic
HOSPITALITY

Library of Congress Control Number: 2010940698

ISBN: 978-0-87197-561-4

Dave Kempf *Publisher*
Mary Lawson *Editor*
LeAnna Massingille *Cover and Layout Designer*

Special thanks to Stan Hardaway—Hardaway Construction; Sandy Dickerson—Earl Swensson Associates, Inc.;
Bill Lockwood—Barge Waggoner Sumner & Cannon, Inc.; E. W. "Bud" Wendell;
Justin Harvey—Nashville Public Television; Beth Odle—Nashville Public Library, Special Collections;
Brenda Colladay—Gaylord Entertainment / Grand Ole Opry; Tom Stanford—The Tennessean

Printed in China

Published by

SW SOUTHWESTERN
Publishing Group®

2451 Atrium Way • Nashville, Tennessee 37214
800-358-0560
www.historichospitalitybooks.com

Introduction

Dear Reader,

In creating the *Historic Hospitality*® series of books, it is our sincere desire, as publisher, to present beautifully crafted books that relate the cherished history of each property, highlight beautiful historic and contemporary photography, and offer delicious recipes unique to the property to make the perfect memoir of your visit or a very special gift for a friend.

We are proud to include the Gaylord Opryland Resort and Convention Center, America's largest non-casino resort, located in Nashville, Tennessee, as one of our featured Historic Hospitality sites. It is our pleasure to share their story with you.

Sincerely,

David J. Kempf

Dave Kempf
Southwestern Publishing Group, Inc.

GAYLORD OPRYLAND RESORT

The Gaylord Opryland Resort and Convention Center is a destination like none other . . . from its nine acres of indoor gardens to its world-class dining options, fabulous shopping, on-site entertainment and 600,000 square feet of meeting and exhibition space all in one location.

WHERE IT ALL BEGAN

Long before there was a magnificent Opryland Hotel gracing the banks of the Cumberland River, the site upon which it now stands was home to prehistoric Indians. They, no doubt, were also drawn to the beauty of this location with its many streams flowing into the river that meandered through Middle Tennessee. Its rich soil and abundance of game presented an ideal place to take up residence, and Native Americans, most likely of the Woodland and Archaic cultures, maintained several villages throughout the area. They eventually mysteriously disappeared, but centuries later, Middle Tennessee was still a hunting ground for the Cherokee Indians. After striking a bargain with them for their claim to the land, the first group of Anglo settlers arrived at the Cumberland Bluff on Christmas Day in 1779. The following spring, some sixty families, including women and children, came in thirty flatboats down the Tennessee River and up the Cumberland. They founded a new community which was renamed as Nashville in 1784. The first school and the first church located west of the Cumberland Mountains were actually constructed just across the river from where the hotel stands today. By 1850, John Pennington had purchased some fourteen hundred acres in one of the bends of the Cumberland River, later known as Pennington Bend, upon which the Gaylord Opryland Resort and Convention Center is built today. The story of its eventual discovery as the future site of the hotel is an intriguing one.

THE MAN WITH THE IDEA

As we fast forward to the early 1960s when Nashville was a thriving metropolis and growing at every level, its plans were in place to encircle the city with a four-lane highway called Briley Parkway. Fortuitously, by the mid-1960s, the section planned through Pennington Bend was nearly complete, and it would unknowingly play an integral part in the evolution of what would become the Opryland Hotel. It was in 1968 that Irving Waugh, a distinguished and delightful man who was president of WSM radio and television in Nashville, which was owner of the world-famous *Grand Ole Opry*, presented his innovative new idea to the finance committee of WSM's parent corporation, the National Life and Accident Insurance Company. Knowing very well that insurance companies welcome wise investment opportunities and inspired by the monopoly of the overwhelmingly successful theme park called Disneyland in California, Waugh presented his idea of a joint venture for WSM and National Life. That venture would be a musical theme park featuring not only country music, for which Nashville was internationally recognized, but include the celebration of American music itself with live stage shows as well as rides, shops, good food, and good times. The committee later approved the proposed theme park and determined that it should include a new Grand Ole Opry House to replace the deteriorating Ryman Auditorium in downtown Nashville and a mini-village called "Oprytown" which would contain commercial shops, restaurants and a two-hundred-room motel, all of which would be called Opryland USA.

FINDING ITS PLACE

Val Smith, a friend of Irving Waugh's and then an assistant vice president in National Life's Mortgage Loan Department was charged with finding a suitable site for the proposed $31 million complex to be known as Opryland USA. He and others were presented with the challenge of searching for a parcel of land that would not only be fairly close to Nashville, but would also have relatively flat terrain and easy accessibility. In addition, it must be large enough to not only support the three initial phases of the complex, but include room for future expansion. It was not until Smith was flying in his private plane over the Nashville area several months later that he noticed the highway construction that soon would be Briley Parkway. There below him was a huge area of farmland just south of the parkway's exit at McGavock Pike ideally located beside the Cumberland River only seven miles from downtown Nashville, which included a parcel of real estate that would eventually total 425 acres. The rest is history. National Life, WSM, and city officials broke ground for Opryland USA on June 30, 1970. On May 27, 1972, the park opened, and shortly afterward, construction of the Grand Ole Opry House was begun. Irving Waugh's dream theme park became a reality and an overwhelming success. 1.5 million happy visitors passed through the gates of the new park during the first season!

THE EVOLUTION BEGINS

Spurred on by the overwhelming response to the new southern mecca, it was clear that another feasibility study would definitely be in order. It was determined that the size of a prospective "Oprytown Motel" be increased to include from four hundred to six hundred rooms with the capability of further expansion. It was further suggested that the site of the present-day Opryland Hotel at the intersection of Briley Parkway and McGavock Pike be set aside for construction of the mini-village, Oprytown, and the adjoining motel. In the fall of 1975, work began to prepare the land for construction of the newly renamed "Opryland Hotel" to more appropriately project its image. In a press release issued the following spring, the enormity of the current project was revealed as follows: "The facility will be comprised of six separate buildings, a three-story 'core' building containing the main lobby, restaurants, shops, a three-and-one-half story galleria covered with a skylight, a ballroom seating up to 2,200 persons with a permanent stage, what may be Nashville's first and largest show lounge, and separate 30,000 square-foot exhibition hall. Five free-standing buildings, ranging from three to five stories in height and connected by enclosed hallways, will provide 601 guest rooms and 14 sitting rooms. The hotel complex has been designed so that it can ultimately be expanded to a total of 1,000 rooms." All in all, it was declared to become "one of, if not, THE largest self-contained convention facilities between Chicago and Miami Beach."

WORKING TOGETHER

Such a monumental project would require a person with years of hotel experience, as well as immense skills and ability to see it through. That man was Jack Vaughn who not only had the experience but the enthusiasm and vision necessary to create a model for the industry. He signed on as general manager in May 1975 and set about his task of designing the hotel's southern plantation theme with a meticulous eye for detail and a vision larger than life. He immediately realized the future hotel's enormous potential to host convention and trade shows and doubled the square footage on its blueprints for this purpose and a building committee was soon appointed. Even before the official announcement confirming the hotel's construction had been made, fifty thousand room nights, totaling almost $3 million in business to future conventions had been sold. Architectural design for the Opryland Hotel was awarded to two Nashville firms: Earl Swensson & Associates and Architect-Engineers Associates, headed by Charles Warterfield, who emphasized that the hotel's design needed to be "a sprawling complex, an expansion of Opryland Park, with the convention-center complex blending into the overall Opryland landscape with its close alliance with nature and open spaces." The addition of the magnificent hotel to its already successful Opryland USA complex was welcomed with excitement. It would be Jack Vaughn who would lead that dream into actuality.

Joint Venture: Earl Swensson, left, and Charles Warterfield are cooperating in the design of the Opryland Hotel. Swensson heads Earl Swensson & Associates; Warterfield's firm is Architects-Engineers Associates.

TWO VISIONARIES

When initially presented with the idea of leading a hotel venture located in a cow pasture in Tennessee, Jack Vaughn was not immediately impressed. He was, after all, enjoying the glamour of Beverly Hills where he was manager of Westin's acclaimed Century Plaza Hotel after spending years working his way up the corporate ladder, literally beginning by parking cars. But his attitude changed after a visit from the Grand Ole Opry's then general manager, E.W. "Bud" Wendell, who convinced Vaughn to travel cross-country to tour the pastureland site. Standing on that land, at a time when hotels were just evolving from a cottage business to an industry, Vaughn's skepticism turned into unbelievable enthusiasm. He already knew that getting many people into the hotels at the same time would one day be the lifeblood of the business, and so he birthed the unique vision of a world-class hotel and convention center incorporating a distinctive plantation theme true to its southern location. In 1975, he took on responsibility for the concept, design, construction, and staffing of the hotel. With the unstoppable inspiration of a man with a mission, the veteran Hotelier directed Opryland Hotel's emergence from the ground up as a world famous, award-winning convention center. In the eyes of many of his peers, he was the greatest hotelier of his time. All would agree with Irving Waugh who is quoted as saying, "In Jack Vaughn, we struck gold."

EXCEEDING EXPECTATIONS

The highly anticipated debut of the Opryland Hotel arrived on November 26, 1977 when its first guests beheld its splendor. The extraordinary circular driveway beautifully emphasized the majestic architectural style reminiscent of the Governor's Palace in colonial Williamsburg, Virginia, and hinted of the treasures within. Together, Jack Vaughn and interior designer, Jerry Law, had meticulously attended to every detail. An enormous breathtaking chandelier hung from the lofty ceiling affirming their hopes of grandeur. Upon entering the spacious Magnolia Lobby, her visitors were no doubt stunned by the magnificent staircase with its hand-turned railings. An elegant carpet made by a British company that bore the seal of the royal family with a pattern dating back to the eighteenth century, covered the stately stairway descending from the mezzanine to the main floor. Down the corridor from the lobby, the discovery of several gift shops, boutiques, restaurants, and bars delighted patrons. The Old Hickory Restaurant, in particular, was exemplary of the elegance and tradition of the Old South. Just past the restaurant on the walls of the lobby of the twenty-thousand-square-foot Tennessee Ballroom was a series of huge ceiling-to-floor murals depicting Nashville in the 1890s. Beneath the ballroom, on the basement level, was an expansive thirty-thousand-square-foot exhibit area ready to extend a traditional southern welcome to conventioneers. The vision of the Opryland Hotel had now become an impressive reality.

THE DREAM TEAM

During its first year of operation, three hundred fifty thousand guests had come through the doors of the Opryland Hotel. In the hotel's second full year, the occupancy rate leaped to 86 percent, largely due to its key staff members, Joe Henry, the resident manager, Margaret Parker, corporate sales manager and former executive secretary to WSM President Irving Waugh, and Mike Dimond, director of sales and marketing, who were part of the energetic team that guided the hotel's ascent to astounding success. Jack Vaughn attributed much of that success to Dimond who with his teammates recruited convention groups from across America. "Mike put the hotel on the map," said Vaughn, and it certainly was. But behind the scenes was Bud Wendell, who had joined National Life in 1950 as an insurance agent and was soon placed in charge of the Ryman Auditorium, and now supported this talented group as president of the Opryland complex, which included the hotel. Jack Vaughn offered this tribute to Wendell, Irving Waugh's successor as follows: "Bud Wendell allowed us to be the success we are. All he had to do was say 'no' to our ideas and they would have vanished. But he allowed us to dream, and gave us the autonomy to succeed or fail." And succeed they did. The hotel was awarded its "Four Star" status by the Mobil Corporation in 1980 and achieved an almost unbelievable 98.9 percent occupancy rate during the summer months of that year.

A GROWING EFFORT
The Garden Conservatory—Phase II

The phenomenal success of the Opryland Hotel during its infancy prompted the National Life officials to purchase the remaining fifty-seven acres between the hotel, McGavock Pike, and the Cumberland River. On April 14, 1981, they were again ready to make public their intention for their first major expansion. The architects for Phase I, Warterfield and Swensson, were again selected to design Phase II. Hardaway Construction, one of the contractors for Phase I, and Sharondale Construction were chosen as builders of the huge project. They would enlarge the hotel by 419 rooms and add two hundred twenty five thousand feet of meeting and exhibition space, including a thirty-thousand-square-foot ballroom. Their banquet facilities would provide more than twice their previous capacity, with the capability of serving as many as fifty-two hundred at a sitting. The hotel's first signature seven-story atrium, the Garden Conservatory, would allow guests to walk in an indoor subtropical garden covered with huge panes of glass without ever going outdoors. Hundreds of rooms with balconies would allow guests to enjoy the view overlooking a stream and a five-story fountain. Target date for completion of Phase II was early 1984, at a price of $40 million. However, in 1983, six years after opening, the hotel had completed its first major expansion which included over one thousand rooms. Even before its completion, a significant change had already taken place. More were waiting in the wings.

THE NEW OWNER

Changes were not only massive in the structure of the hotel complex, but in its ownership. Both WSM-FM and National Life had already been sold. Even before Phase II of the Opryland Hotel's expansion was completed, while workmen were still putting the finishing touches on the 1.5 acre Garden Conservatory, the announcement was made that a new owner had purchased the Opryland complex itself for a reported $240 million. That new owner was Edward L. Gaylord, an Oklahoma City businessman whose family had inherited the major Oklahoma City metro newspaper, Daily Oklahoman and other assets worth $50 million. His sizable holdings at the time of the purchase of the Opryland complex in July 1983 included radio and TV stations, and daily newspapers across the country. Those holdings now included the expanding Opryland Hotel, the *Grand Ole Opry*, The Nashville Network, and Country Music Television. Ed Gaylord made it clear from the beginning that there were no plans for dramatic changes in Opryland's management and that he intended to keep Bud Wendell at the helm of his new acquisition. To emphasize that point, he purchased a full-page ad in the Wall Street Journal that stated: "On the day the papers were signed, an elegant lady from Grinder's Switch, Tennessee, Miss Minnie Pearl, very wisely told us, 'If it ain't broke, don't fix it.' It ain't, so we won't. It doesn't need fixing."

OVERFLOWING SUCCESS
The Cascades—Phase III

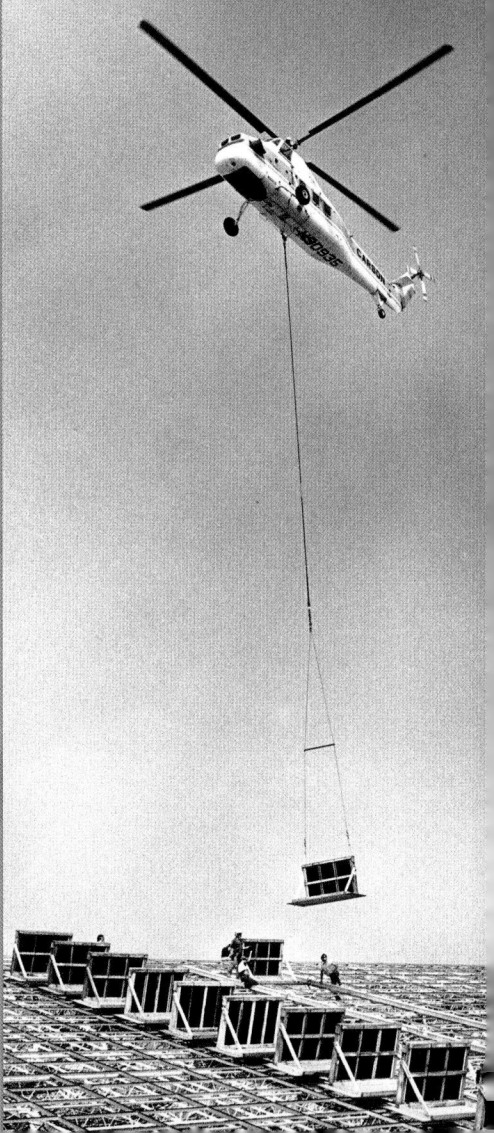

The expansion plans continued their momentum and even as Phase II had just formally opened in 1983, Bud Wendell announced that a new building project was a serious consideration. The formal announcement of specific plans for Phase III was made on October 22, 1985. It would add 700 guest rooms (later expanded to 824), six meeting rooms, and forty thousand square feet of exhibit space, a ballroom, as well as shops, and a spectacular waterscape called the Cascades. Construction would begin in early 1986 at a projected cost of $55 million. The hotel would then be one of the largest hostelries in the country. Meanwhile, the new Garden Conservatory with its four waterfalls surrounded by meandering paths and benches to attract visitors through its luscious gardens was the talk of the town and a hit with hundreds of out-of-town guests who lodged at the hotel daily. By mid-1987, Phase III was well underway with its Cascades, a six-story atrium covered by an acre of glass that promised to be another phenomenal attraction of the Opryland Hotel. The installation of three thousand huge glass panes in the 328 × 165-foot skylight over the two-acre indoor garden was an enormous challenge requiring helicopter service that would transport crates of glass from the ground to the top of the building. The magnanimous, yet tedious, effort was carried out without the loss of a single pane.

STATISTICALLY SPEAKING

The remarkable Cascades atrium with its 824 surrounding rooms was completed in the spring of 1988. The ambience was one of an island paradise, complete with cascading waterfalls, a 12,500-square-foot lake, and tropical plants soaking up the sun's rays that poured through the colossal dome of glass. A revolving lounge housed in an extravagant gazebo providing the perfect place to enjoy a spectacular light and music show—all this with a restaurant and additional meeting and exhibit space for a mere $55 million. With expansion now the necessary trend, in 1991 nearly thirty-nine thousand more feet of meeting and office space at a cost of $3.1 million was completed, and Gaylord Entertainment announced that the company would go public with an offering of nine million shares of stock valued at approximately $200 million. All nine million shares were sold on the first day of trading. It was in 1992 after the hotel's first fifteen years in operation that the statistics were released. Since its opening, 9.3 million guests had stayed overnight, while more than 25 million people had walked its halls. It boasted the largest exhibit facility inside a hotel in all of North America and, based on the number of guest rooms, the Opryland Hotel was now America's twelfth largest.

BRINGING THE OUTSIDE IN

The Delta—Phase IV

The largest single project in Nashville's history came about with Gaylord's next major announcement. In May 1993, the plans for Phase IV with an investment of nearly $200 million were made public. Amazingly, the Opryland Hotel had turned away four hundred fifty thousand guests over the past four years for lack of space, so Jack Vaughn announced that this expansion would add 979 guest rooms, bringing the total number to 2,884, and the exhibit space would grow to three hundred thousand square feet. The most delightful news, however, to anyone and everyone who followed the rise of the hotel was the creation of a new, glass-covered arboretum, much larger than the Conservatory and Cascades. To be built in the style reminiscent of New Orleans, the new Delta would cover 4.5 acres and include an indoor river stretching more than a quarter-mile and equipped with flatboats to transport passengers on a ten-minute pleasure cruise complete with waterfalls. An amphitheater, restaurants, and a village of shops would also delight its visitors. In addition, it was no small matter that locals would benefit from this huge endeavor that created some thirteen hundred jobs and an additional payroll of almost $25 million. The culmination of the gigantic effort would not be until three years later, but it was well worth the wait.

PHENOMENAL ACHIEVEMENTS

The Opryland Hotel completed its Phase IV expansion in 1996 which more than doubled the size of the existing structure. A lake system with two waterfalls and a fountain with jets that shot water eighty-five feet up toward the one-hundred-fifty-foot-tall Delta Dome awaited the anticipative visitors. When the longest indoor waterway in the world was christened, water samples from more than seventeen hundred rivers throughout the world, including every registered river in the United States, were poured into the Delta River. A variety of trees and flowers filled the atrium and lined the waterway, the result of much hard work by the hotel's director of horticulture, Hollis Malone, and his staff of gardeners. It was no small effort. The task of successfully planting three hundred seventy full-grown trees weighing as much as sixteen tons each and up to forty feet tall was monumental. The lovely Delta, inspired by the lure of New Orleans, was a dream come true and an added incentive to convention planners. Not only did it have twenty new meeting rooms and almost one thousand new guest rooms, but its outstanding attraction was the new 1.5 acre ballroom with a seating capacity of five thousand. The Opryland Hotel now housed the four largest ballrooms in Tennessee and had gained the distinguished title of the largest combined hotel/convention center under one roof anywhere.

A TIME OF TRANSITION

With the completion of the Delta expansion, a new sense of direction had been solidified. It was clear with the company boasting annual revenues of $500 million and assets of over $1 billion that Gaylord Entertainment was moving in the right direction. Its focus on the hotel and conventions was, without a doubt, a winner. In May 1997, new management was charged with the streamlining of operations upon Bud Wendell's retirement as president and CEO of Gaylord after forty-seven years with Gaylord and National Life. Since the massive Opryland Hotel had now assumed a starring role and left no more room for the Opryland theme park to expand, a decision was made to emphasize the lodging portion of its multi-faceted business ventures. Only recently, the company had announced it would sell two of its Nashville-based holdings, The Nashville Network (TNN) and Country Music Television (CMT). By mid-summer 1997, the Gaylord team was exploring options for the Opryland Park site and, in early November, an announcement was made that the park would be replaced by a giant 1.2-million-square-foot, two-hundred-million-dollar retail and entertainment mall consisting of two hundred stores and restaurants and would be called Opry Mills. Opryland USA closed and was dismantled following the 1997 season in lieu of the new focus. Ultimately, Gaylord divested its share of the mall and now leases the property.

THE GREAT FLOOD OF 2010

Historic torrential rains in May 2010, resulted in a devastating flood that left parts of the Opryland hotel, at one point, under ten feet of water and destroyed much of its common area. With the rising waters, the Gaylord Opryland employees rose to the occasion. The accounts of individual heroic efforts by a dedicated staff could fill a book. In an effort to give back to the community while under devastating assault themselves, employee volunteers loaded tens of thousands of pounds of perishable food onto refrigerated trucks to be donated to organizations to assist with emergency feeding of area flood victims. A veritable army of contractors on site worked together to restore the hotel and redesign the Cascades lobby, the Cascades American Café Restaurant, and the Cascades Terrace Bar, as well as the Volare and Jack Daniel's Restaurants, the Magnolia guest rooms, and the presidential suites. An entire city of infrastructure which operates under the Gaylord Opryland campus, the majority of which was fully under water including offices, electrical, IT, and mechanical required the relocation of many employees into a temporary trailer city during the restoration efforts. Other members of Gaylord's iconic entertainment family suffered damage as well, including the Wildhorse Saloon, but the most significant was to the Grand Ole Opry House, which required replacement of the majority of its ground floor. With incredible resilience, however, and months of intensive reconstruction, the Gaylord Opryland Resort began an exciting new chapter in its Nashville story and came back better than ever!

2010 Flood Recovery

A NEW LEGACY

Since its first Four Star rating in 1980, the Gaylord Opryland Resort has continued to garner the most prestigious awards in the hospitality industry, largely due to the vision of its leaders. In 2001, at a time when the operation needed sharper focus, Colin Reed was named chief executive officer of Gaylord Entertainment and proceeded to strategically create an iconic company through emphasis on large meetings and conventions with "a destination" in mind. That strategy set the precedent for the pioneering of Gaylord's network of upscale, meetings-focused resorts in Kissimmee, Florida (Orlando area), Grapevine, Texas (Dallas area), and National Harbor, Maryland (Washington DC area) and established them as a leading hospitality and entertainment company. Locally in Nashville, with ownership of the Ryman Auditorium and the Grand Ole Opry in hand, Reed catered to the emotional connections people have long felt about the legendary home of country music itself. With the largest structural hotel in the world and its six hundred thousand square feet of meeting and exhibition space and nearly three thousand guest rooms, the Gaylord Opryland Resort and Convention Center can accommodate virtually any convention in North America while providing the ideal business and leisure destination. Equally impressive is the dedication to flawless service by its employees, an abundance of shops, inviting restaurants with a cuisine for every taste, the longest indoor river in the world, and gardened walkways under year-round, climate-controlled atriums. It is indeed a destination like no other.

THE NASHVILLE EXPERIENCE

Though one needn't leave the sprawling Opryland complex, the flagship of Gaylord Entertainment's "best in class" line of hotels to enjoy an unforgettable stay, a visit to Gaylord's other local iconic entertainment venues will complete your experience. The opportunity to see the world-famous Ryman Auditorium, still going strong after more than eighty years of producing music history and named one of "America's 21 Wonders" by Life Magazine in 2007 should not be missed. Equally as exciting is a visit to the crown jewel of country music, the *Grand Ole Opry*, whose weekly performances can be heard on over two hundred radio stations across the United States and on the Armed Forces Radio Network. Other memorable experiences include a trip on Gaylord's General Jackson Showboat and a visit to the Wildhorse Saloon. The unique story of each one weaves in and out of the history of the hotel itself and is briefly related in the following pages. (We have also included four recipes from the resort's Old Hickory Steakhouse, a Nashville destination in its own right, to enjoy upon your return home.) Each venue is a vital part of the history of Nashville, a city hailed by *Travel & Leisure* magazine as one of the "friendliest cities in the United States" and a city that is unlike no other. Don't miss your opportunity to experience all that is Music City!

RYMAN AUDITORIUM

The Ryman Auditorium is synonymous with country music and Nashville, Tennessee. As a National Historic Landmark, it represents more than one hundred years of history and music tradition. The auditorium first opened as the Union Gospel Tabernacle in 1892 as a vision of a boisterous Thomas G. Ryman, who, ironically, owned several saloons and built the church for an influential revivalist named Samuel Porter Jones. Captain Ryman had disrupted Jones's services but then experienced a religious conversion, which may explain his generosity. After Ryman's death, the building was renamed for him. By the turn of the century the Ryman had become one of the South's premier performance halls and showcased a wide variety of entertainment genres whose stars included the biggest names in music such as opera star Rudolph Valentino and famed composer Edward Strauss as well as other legendary stars such as Mae West, W. C. Fields, Will Rogers, and Charlie Chaplin. When the Ryman Auditorium became the home of the famed *Grand Ole Opry* in 1943 it gained nationwide recognition as the "Mother Church of Country Music" featuring pioneering performers including Bill Monroe, Hank Williams, and Patsy Cline who helped shape the future of country and bluegrass music. In 1974, the Opry moved from the decaying Ryman to its current home at the Grand Ole Opry House owned by Gaylord Entertainment. In 1994, the Ryman was completely renovated and is a must-see for thousands of Nashville visitors.

GRAND OLE OPRY

Part I

Good Housekeeping magazine said it best in a 1954 article exclaiming "The Mecca of all country and Western music lovers is Nashville, Tennessee, where the famous radio program *Grand Ole Opry* originates." That statement still stands true today. The *Grand Ole Opry* started as the WSM *Barn Dance* with "hillbilly music" in the new radio station studio of the National Life & Accident Insurance Company in downtown Nashville on November 28, 1925 with George D. Hay, then known as the most popular radio announcer in America. Hay had been recruited from WLS-AM in Chicago and is credited with suggesting its ultimate name. Called "the biggest hoedown in the history of hoedowns" in 1955 by a national magazine, the show's regulars included the Possum Hunters, the Fruit Jar Drinkers as well as square dancers. In 1926, Uncle Dave Macon, a Tennessee banjo player who had toured the vaudeville circuit, became its first real star. As audiences for the live show increased, its radio venue became too small to accommodate the hordes of fans. After a few temporary moves to other buildings about town, on June 5, 1943, the Opry found its home in what is now known as the Ryman Auditorium where one magazine's description of the show's appeal was, "It usually plays to a packed house of three and a half thousand with another one or two thousand waiting outside for vacant seats."

GRAND OLE OPRY
Part II

For thirty-one years, the Opry stayed at the Ryman accruing a terrible state of disrepair in the process. With no air conditioning, substandard restrooms, a leaking roof, and uncomfortable pews, it was apparent that America's favorite radio program would again need a new home. The audiences that enjoyed country music legends such as Ernest Tubb, Hank Williams, Bill Monroe, Patsy Cline, Minnie Pearl, Loretta Lynn, Johnny Cash, George Jones, and Tammy Wynette, would soon enjoy the comfort of a new facility to be built in the new Opryland USA theme park nine miles east of Nashville where their favorite stars could be seen on television as well. In 1974, the show moved to the forty-four hundred seat Grand Ole Opry House. On the opening night of March 16, President Nixon joined the celebration by playing a few songs on the piano on the stage that included an inlaid circle five feet in diameter that had been removed from the Ryman stage's original floor. Since then, the weekly concerts dedicated to honoring country music and its history have presented hundreds of performers including new stars, superstars, and legends such as Dolly Parton, Reba McEntire, Garth Brooks, Alan Jackson, and Vince Gill, to name a few. This American icon, "the show that made Country Music famous," with its ⸻⸻ one-hour "barn dance," now attracts hundreds of thousands of ⸻⸻ ⸻⸻ and internet listeners.

GRANDOLEOPRY®

SIMPLY UNFORGETTABLE

Two country music icons, whose honored images cast in bronze are seated together in lasting tribute at the Ryman Auditorium, were not only Opry stars for decades, but were the closest of friends. Roy Acuff was known as "The King of Country Music," and Minnie Pearl was one of the most widely recognized comic performers American culture has ever produced. In the years just prior to World War II, they individually found their way to the Opry stage, each offering their own unique contributions to the show, ensuring their place as entertainment legends and paving the way for lifetime friendship. Roy Acuff became the Opry's greatest star, introducing enduring songs such as "Great Speckled Bird," "Wabash Cannonball" and "Blue Eyes Crying in the Rain." He also published "The Tennessee Waltz" through his Acuff-Rose Publishing Company formed to promote his popular Opry songs. Minnie Pearl appeared on the *Grand Ole Opry* for more than fifty years and on the television show *Hee Haw* from 1970 to 1991. Her unforgettable hollered "Howdeee" always announced her stage entrance before she lovingly satirized rural America while wearing a straw hat with its dangling $1.98 price tag as her trademark. In reality, the humor she brought to all of us as country music's preeminent comedian is priceless. In the words of E.W. "Bud" Wendell, retired President and CEO of Gaylord Entertainment, "Roy Acuff and Minnie Pearl were the *Grand Ole Opry*."

OPRYLAND ART

From the beginning, the Opryland Hotel embraced the art of Tennessee artists and welcomed it as a reflection of Nashville's history and its people. Shortly after the hotel's opening, an art competition was held to obtain the best renditions for its permanent collection, resulting in fifty-three pieces which formed the basis of the Hotel's "Tennessee Art Collection." A second competition was held in 1991 and another in 1997, which brought the number of artworks to 175. On an even larger scale, the centerpiece of the hotel's artworks, ceiling-to-floor murals on the walls of the Tennessee Ballroom lobby depicting the history of Nashville in the 1880s and 1890s, are literally "another story." In 1976, Max Hochstetler, an associate art professor at Tennessee's Austin Peay State University, with no experience in murals, was commissioned to take on the grandiose project consisting of over twenty-two hundred square feet of wall space divided into ten-foot units attached in mural fashion to the walls. Seven students assisted him on the murals, done in sections like strips of wallpaper using over two hundred yards of canvas. Hochstetler created scenes on his renderings of historic places populating them with the faces of people he knew, even including himself in one of the panels—appropriately, as a sign painter. The murals that "sign painter" created stands as a lasting tribute to some of Nashville's most loved landmarks, including Nashville's old public square and Union Station.

GENERAL JACKSON SHOWBOAT

During the time of the construction of the Cascades at the Opryland Hotel, a most unique attraction reminiscent of the Old South was added to the Opryland theme park. The General Jackson Showboat, built in the grand tradition of its predecessors who traveled the waterways of the Mississippi and Ohio rivers in the nineteenth century made its grand debut. Showboats had long been a colorful part of our nation's history and though their popularity had declined before the Civil War, by 1878 they were again delighting their audiences with new emphasis on vaudeville and melodramas. Enter the three-hundred-foot paddlewheel riverboat, the General Jackson, to continue that tradition at the park by delighting its audiences in true *Showboat* fashion with live musical entertainment. On April 20, 1985, it was launched on the Cumberland River in Nashville as one of the largest showboats in the country. Built by the largest inland shipbuilder in the United States, Jeffboat, located in Indiana, its reminiscent design resembles a vintage steam-powered riverboat complete with paddlewheel. The boat has a capacity of twelve hundred passengers and 157 crew members. Though the park closed in 1997, it carries on the riverboat tradition as a signature attraction of Gaylord Entertainment, with its four massive decks and a beautiful two-story Victorian Theater located in the center of the boat, in which livemusicals are performed while passengers dine in luxury "rollin' down the river" between the hotel and downtown Nashville.

WILDHORSE SALOON

During the continual expansion work on the site of the Opryland Hotel, Gaylord continued to widen its presence in an appreciative Nashville. It purchased and razed a decaying warehouse on historic Second Avenue downtown, an area greatly in need of refurbishing and built the Wildhorse Saloon. The exciting new tri-level, sixty-six-thousand-square-foot combination country dance hall and nightclub, would be a live music and dance destination attracting newcomers from across America. On June 1, 1994, country superstar Reba McIntyre herded a stampede of live cattle through the streets of Music City and past the front doors of the newly opened club to boldly emphasize its arrival. The top two levels of the Wildhorse overlook the largest dance floor in the world, at a total 4,982 square feet. As such, it initially capitalized on the line dancing craze of the early- to mid-1990s and formerly hosted the *Wildhorse Saloon Dance Show* on The Nashville Network and has now been involved in thousands of TV shows and tapings. Currently, the Wildhorse Saloon is a concert site and dance venue for the thousands of music lovers who visit Nashville. In addition, its restaurant, the largest per capita restaurant in all of Tennessee, with its enticing award-winning menu is an attraction unto itself. Annually, more than 1.5 million music fans come to the Wildhorse to have a great meal, catch the hottest concerts, and learn the newest dance steps.

A COUNTRY CHRISTMAS

In the weeks before Christmas, the Opryland Hotel transforms into a winter wonderland for the thousands of people who travel from around the world to experience the most captivating holiday resort entertainment, décor, and food in America. The cherished tradition first began on December 7, 1984, when "A Country Christmas" included local Christmas carolers, an art and craft show, a miniature Christmas village, holiday storytelling sessions with *Grand Ole Opry* stars and a major musical production. By 1995, the event had become one of complete enchantment and an annual must-see for thousands of visitors who returned year after year. Today, the Nashville holiday tradition lasts over six weeks. The thousands of lights that decorated a fifty-foot Christmas tree at the hotel's entrance that first year in 1984 are now over two million in number creating a magical holiday wonderland inside and out. With each passing year, the shows and attractions have increased to more than a dozen and include everything from horse-drawn carriage rides to Christmas dinner shows aboard the General Jackson Showboat. Christmas music and entertainment at the complex ranges from live bands to the Radio City Christmas Spectacular featuring the Radio City Rockettes. Graced by the world's largest nativity display and a walk-through winter wonderland carved from two million pounds of ice, a visit to Gaylord Opryland offers the memories of a lifetime.

Christmas at Opryland

GAYLORD SPRINGS GOLF LINKS

With attention focused on providing first-class amenities for its tourists and conventioneers, the addition of a world-class golf course was exciting news from the continually expanding Gaylord Opryland Hotel and Resort. Available land for such an endeavor was rapidly depleting, so two hundred twenty acres on the east side of Briley Parkway, a short distance from the hotel, was purchased from a nearby landowner. In August 1988, Gaylord Entertainment announced that Larry Nelson, a U.S. Open and two-time PGA champion, would be the designer of their Springhouse Golf Club, later named for the century-old springhouse that would be located at its signature fourth hole. Carved from the historic banks of the Cumberland River and designed in Scottish links-style, the beautiful par seventy-two layout offers eighteen challenging holes enhanced by federally protected wetlands and bordered by limestone bluffs. With a long list of awards, Gaylord Springs Golf Links has earned its place among the nation's best golf courses.

OLD HICKORY LOBSTER BISQUE

3	half-pound live female lobsters
2	carrots, peeled and small diced
3	stalks celery, small diced
4	medium shallots, small diced
2	cloves garlic, peeled and minced
3/4	cup vegetable oil
1	tbsp chopped fresh tarragon
4	ounces Brandy

1	cup heavy cream
1	cup white wine
2 1/2	quarts lobster stock
1	6 ounce can tomato paste
5	Yukon Gold Potatoes, peeled and cut into chunks
	cracked black pepper
	salt

Cut the lobster down the center of the head between the eyes and leave the tail whole. Separate the tail, the head, and remove the claws. Keep any shells, juices, the tomalley and the roe in a bowl and refrigerate. Heat a stockpot on high heat and add the oil. Sear the cut pieces of lobster cut side down, and add the tail and claws whole. Cook until the shells are bright red and the flesh is almost cooked, about eight minutes. Crush the shells with a spoon to extract more flavor.

Remove lobster from the pan and set to the side. Add oil to the pan and sauté the shallots, carrot, celery, and garlic until lightly browned. Add tomato paste and sauté for two minutes. Add white wine, and brandy and cook for three minutes, whisking to evenly disperse the tomato. Add lobster stock and cream. Add herbs and lobster shells to the pot and bring to a boil, skimming any froth or fat with a four-ounce ladle. Simmer for twenty minutes.

Add the potatoes and cook for additional twenty minutes. Remove lobster and set aside. Add reserved lobster juices, tomalley, roe and chopped tarragon, and whisk until smooth. Simmer for fifteen minutes. Strain through a fine strainer using a ladle or rubber spatula to force as much as possible through it.

Remove meat from lobster and cut into bite size chunks. Serve with meat.

Yields: 8 Servings

BLUE CHEESE AU GRATIN

1   pound Yukon Potatoes, peeled and sliced 1/4 inch
     thick
1   onion, Julienne cut
2   tbsp Thyme, fresh picked and chopped
2   cups heavy cream
1/2 cup shredded Parmesan Cheese
1   cup crumbled blue cheese
     salt and freshly ground pepper

Preheat oven to 375 degrees. Butter a 9 x 13-inch baking dish or similar sized casserole dish. Combine the potatoes, cream, onion, and thyme in a bowl. Season with salt and pepper and toss all ingredients. Place half of potato mixture in baking dish and spread half the blue cheese and Parmesan over the potatoes. Add remaining potatoes and sprinkle the rest of the cheese on top.

Press down on the mixture to compact being careful that cream does not overflow. Cover with foil and bake for one and a half hours. Remove foil and bake another fifteen minutes until browned. To ensure that potatoes are totally cooked, insert a knife and feel for resistance. Let set for ten minutes, and then serve.

Yields: 4 Servings

OLD HICKORY CRÈME BRÛLÉE

1   quart heavy cream
2   vanilla beans
     (split lengthwise)
6   egg yolks
2   cups granulated sugar

Preheat oven to 225 degrees. Place heavy cream and split vanilla beans in a saucepot and bring to a boil. In a mixing bowl, combine the egg yolks and sugar. When cream comes to a boil, remove from heat and add about 2 ounces of the cream to the egg and sugar mixture. (Keep whisking to prevent the egg from scrambling.) Add two more ounces of the cream and continue whisking. Add the remaining cream to the bowl. Let sit for about one hour, or longer, to let the vanilla flavor infuse to the cream.

Fill a crème brûlée dish (or a shallow coffee cup) almost to the top. Place inside a larger casserole dish and fill with water so the water comes half way up the crème brûlée dish. Bake for about one hour until mixture sets and achieves a pudding consistency (a little more time may be necessary.) Let cool.

When ready to serve, add just enough sugar in the raw to cover the top of the custard. Using a torch, caramelize the top.

Yields: 4 six-ounce servings

PRIME NEW YORK STRIP STEAK
With a Red Wine and Blue Cheese Butter

2	16-ounce prime New York strip steaks coarse salt, to taste		pepper to taste
		4	tbsp red wine and blue cheese butter (recipe below)

Preheat a clean well-greased grill to medium-high heat. Season steaks liberally with salt and pepper on all sides and grill on each side approximately four minutes. (For a medium-rare, turn once to ensure even charring.) Remove steaks from grill for five minutes. Top with butter two minutes before serving and enjoy.

RED WINE AND BLUE CHEESE BUTTER

1	shallot, minced	1	pound unsalted butter, room temperature
1	sprig thyme, leaves removed and chopped	1/2	pound blue cheese, crumbled
3 1/2	cups red wine (Cabernet or Syrah)	1/2	cup chives, minced
3/4	cup demi-glace or a good beef stock		

In a small heavy-bottomed saucepot, heat a tablespoon of butter on low. Once the butter bubbles, sweat shallot and thyme until translucent. Add the wine to the pan and bring to a simmer. Simmer for five minutes. Add demi-glace and continue to simmer for three minutes. Remove from heat and let cool. In a stand-up mixer, whip the butter while slowly adding the red wine mixture, cheese, and chives. (The butter can be made ahead of time and stored in a freezer for up to four weeks.)

Yields: 2 to 4 servings

GAYLORD OPRYLAND®

RESORT & CONVENTION CENTER

Nashville

For More Information, Reservations, and Event Planning

888.777.6779 | Main Hotel Line: 615.889.1000 | Sales Office: 615.458.2800

GAYLORD OPRYLAND
RESORT & CONVENTION CENTER

2800 Opryland Drive, Nashville, Tennessee 37214
www.gaylordhotels.com

DESCRIPTIONS OF PHOTOGRAPHS

Unless otherwise noted, photographic images are provided courtesy of Gaylord Opryland. Those images provided by the Nashville Public Library, Special Collections are indentified by NPL-SC, and those contributed by Hardaway Construction are identified by HC.